You Are Enough

by Ronnie Walter

©2020 Ronnie Walter

All Rights Reserved.

Book layout, illustrations and photographs
©Ronnie Walter

No part of this book can be reproduced, scanned or distributed in any printed or electronic form without permission of the author.

The Coloring Cafe-You Are Enough/Ronnie Walter
ISBN: 978-0-9971595-6-1

Welcome to The Coloring Café™!

Hello!
I drew the "You are Enough" coloring book with you in mind and included this message on each page. Sometimes bold, sometimes subtle (just like the women you)! These pages range from easy designs to color to more complicated, but all were drawn with love, respect, and for a reminder of how amazing you are, just as you are.

I recommend using fine tipped markers, colored pencils, watercolor pencils or pan watercolors. All can be found at any local craft store or online. A heavy application of paint can make the paper buckle a bit so I would use a light hand when using water based paints. Some of the details could be difficult to capture with crayons, but you can certainly use them if you prefer. If you use markers, slip a scrap piece of paper between the pages in case of bleed-through.

Remember, coloring should be relaxing and that includes relaxing your expectation for perfection. My drawings are quirky and certainly not perfect, but I love making them. My intention is to provide you an opportunity to find a calm and pleasant moment in your day. So enjoy!

Thank you so much!

Ronnie

P.S. If you'd like to share your work on social media, please use the hashtag #coloringcafe so we can all enjoy your masterpieces!

www.thecoloringcafe.com

More books from The Coloring Café!

The Coloring Cafe-Volume One
The Coloring Cafe-Volume Two
The Coloring Cafe-To Go! A travel size coloring book!
The Coloring Cafe-Inspired Heart
The Coloring Cafe-Bible Blessings to Color
The Coloring Café-Stress Relief
The Coloring Café-Fashion Girls
The Coloring Café-Paper Dolls to Color
The Coloring Cafe-Coloring Christmas
The Coloring Cafe-Happy Times
The Coloring Cafe-You've Got This, Girl!
The Coloring Cafe-Everyday Angels
The Coloring Cafe-Affirmations
Cuppa Calm-An Inspirational Coloring Journal
Cuppa Cute-A Fashion Inspired Coloring Journal

From CQ Publishing:

The Coloring Café-It's a Girl Thing
The Coloring Café-My Cup Runneth Over
The Coloring Café-Happy Everything
The Coloring Café- Kindness Matters
The Coloring Café-Relax, Unwind and Color
The Coloring Café-Life is Delicious
The Colorful Café-Colorful Blessings
The Coloring Cafe-Home is Where it All Begins
The Coloring Café-Be the Sunshine

About The Artist

Ronnie Walter is an artist and award winning writer. She licenses her illustrations on all kinds of products including stickers, greeting cards, stationery, giftware, fabric and more.

Besides the creator of The Coloring Cafe series of adult coloring books, Ronnie is the author of *License to Draw! How to Monetize your Art through Art Licensing...and more!* and *Gruesome Greetings, A Georgie Hardtman Mystery,* both available in paperback and Kindle.

Ronnie lives in paradise with her husband Jim Marcotte and the best shelter dog ever, Larry.

Email: coloringcafe@gmail.com
Facebook: Coloring Cafe
Instagram: @thecoloringcafe #ronniescoloringcafe
Twitter: @thecoloringcafe

www.thecoloringcafe.com

Test your colors here:

Made in the USA
Las Vegas, NV
02 May 2021